Collins English Library

Series editors: K R Cripwell and Lewis Jones

A library of graded readers for students of English as a foreign language, and for reluctant native readers. The books are graded in six levels of difficulty. Structure, vocabulary, idiom and sentence length are all controlled according to principles laid down in detail in *A Teacher's Guide to Collins English Library*. The books are listed below according to level. Level 1 has a basic

The Mystery of Dr Fu Manchu *Sax Rohmer*

Level Three

Climb a Lonely Hill *Lilith Norman*
Custer's Gold *Kenneth Ulyatt*
Gunshot Grand Prix *Douglas Rutherford*
David Copperfield* *Charles Dickens*
Born Free *Joy Adamson*

Five Ghost Stories* *Viola Huggins*
Three English Kings *from Shakespeare*
An American Tragedy *Theodore Dreiser*
Six American Stories* *N Wymer*
Emma and I *Sheila Hocken*
Little Women *Louisa M Alcott*
The Picture of Dorian Gray* *Oscar Wilde*
Maimunah *David Hill*
Marilyn Monroe *Peter Dainty*
Bruce Springsteen *Toni Murphy*
Is That It? *Bob Geldof*
Short Stories *Oscar Wilde*
A Room with a View *E M Forster*
The Importance of Being Ernest *Oscar Wilde*
The Lost World *Sir Arthur Conan Doyle*
Arab Folk Tales *Helen Thomson*
Computers: From Beads to Bytes *Peter Dewar*

Level Four

The White South *Hammond Innes*
A Christmas Carol *Charles Dickens*
King Solomon's Mines* *H Rider Haggard*
Jane Eyre *Charlotte Brontë*
Pride and Prejudice *Jane Austen*
Dr Jekyll and Mr Hyde* *R L Stevenson*
Huckleberry Finn *Mark Twain*
Landslide *Desmond Bagley*
Nothing is the Number When You Die *Joan Fleming*
The African Child *Camara Laye*
The Lovely Lady and other Stories *D H Lawrence*
Airport International *Brian Moynahan*
The Secret Sharer and other Sea Stories *Joseph Conrad*
Death in Vienna? *K E Rowlands*
Hostage Tower* *Alistair MacLean*
The Potter's Wheel *Chukwuemeka Ike*
Tina Turner *Stephen Rabley*
Campbell's Kingdom *Hammond Innes*

Level Five

The Guns of Navarone *Alistair MacLean*
Geordie *David Walker*
Wuthering Heights *Emily Brontë*
Where Eagles Dare *Alistair MacLean*
Wreck of the Mary Deare *Hammond Innes*
I Know My Love *Catherine Gaskin*
Among the Elephants *Iain and Oria Douglas-Hamilton*
The Mayor of Casterbridge *Thomas Hardy*
Sense and Sensibility *Jane Austen*
The Eagle has Landed *Jack Higgins*
Middlemarch *George Eliot*
Victory *Joseph Conrad*
Experiences of Terror* *Roland John*
Japan: Islands in the Mist *Peter Milward*

Level Six

Doctor Zhivago *Boris Pasternak*
The Glory Boys *Gerald Seymour*
In the Shadow of Man *Jane Goodall*
Harry's Game *Gerald Seymour*
House of a Thousand Lanterns *Victoria Holt*
Hard Times *Charles Dickens*
Sons and Lovers *D H Lawrence*
The Dark Frontier *Eric Ambler*
Vanity Fair *William Thackeray*
Inspector Ghote Breaks an Egg *H R F Keating*

Collins English Library Level 5

PETER MILWARD

JAPAN

ISLANDS IN THE MIST

COLLINS
E·L·T

Published in Great Britain by
William Collins Sons and Co Ltd
Glasgow G4 0NB

Printed and published in Great Britain by
William Collins Sons and Co Ltd
Glasgow G4 0NB

First published in the Collins English Library 1984
Reprinted: 1987, 1990

ISBN 0 00 370155 7

Cover illustration by Japan Airlines
Cover design by Dan Lim
Text photographs by the Japan National Tourist
Organisation
We would also like to thank Connoisseur Films Ltd for
permission to reproduce the photograph on
pages 80 and 81.
We would like to thank Hodder and Stoughton
Educational for permission to reproduce the tables of *Kana*
on pages 20 and 21.

Contents

Chapter One
The Islands and the Islanders

"Japan at last!" At last, after so many days at sea, we caught sight of land. It seemed a long time since we had left Manila, our last port of call in Asia. And now we were moving at last into Tokyo Bay.

The land appeared faintly on either side of the ship. It was partly hidden in mist. The weather was unusually cool for that time of the year, early September. But for us, the sight of the land was enough. We had been waiting for this ever since we had left Southampton, England, six weeks before.

To the left of us we saw mountains in the distance. The shape of one of them clearly stood out from the others. Its slopes were so smooth and regular. Could it be? Yes, it was none other than the holy mountain of the Japanese, Mount Fuji!

Yes, we had come to Japan – at least, we were in sight of Japan – on the first of September, 1954. We had come by ship all the way from

England; it was still the old days, before air travel became common. Today, you leave England one day and arrive in Japan the next day. It is *too* sudden! But in those days it was a gradual experience for us. Before reaching Japan we had stopped at many sea-ports in Europe and Asia on the way. And each of them had had its own special interest.

Now at last we had come to our journey's end, Yokohama. We expected this to be the most interesting sea-port of all. In all the sea-ports in Asia we had found another world. Each had been so different from our familiar English world. And now we were approaching the farthest sea-port in the farthest land from England.

At first, however, we were disappointed. We were informed we would arrive that evening; and we did arrive that evening. But by then it was too late to go ashore. We had to spend the night waiting outside the harbour. It was such a long wait, almost longer (we felt) than the whole journey from Southampton. But at last the day dawned. When we woke up, we were free to go ashore.

Once again "At last!" At last, we set foot on Japanese soil. But once again, under a cold grey sky, we felt disappointment. It was raining, but we didn't mind the rain so much. It was what we saw that disappointed us. Here was just another sea-port, not unlike Southampton. It wasn't at all what we were expecting.

We had a long wait for our belongings. They had first to pass through customs, after they were brought ashore. So we had plenty of time to look round the harbour area. It was so much like any other harbour, even in England. But the buildings were all in need of repair, and the roads were full of holes. After all, ten years hadn't yet passed since the end of the war. What we saw was still the old Japan, or the ruins of old Japan.

The signs on the buildings were all written in strange characters. In their silence, they told us we were indeed in Japan. Some of them were written downwards, and others were written across – almost as in a crossword puzzle. They were certainly a puzzle for us!

Then, we noticed the people working in the harbour area. Most of them were small in size, as I expected, but they weren't so yellow. People sometimes speak of the Japanese as a yellow race; but these were mostly brown, no doubt after a hot summer. Some Japanese women who passed us seemed almost pink, like English women.

In the faces of these Japanese, I especially noticed their eyes and their noses. Their eyes were narrow and wide apart. Their noses were so short, they hardly seemed to have any. And then, they were so silent. They reminded me of a society of ever-busy insects.

Meanwhile, some friends had come to meet us

in an old car. Today we are so used to Japanese cars. They are everywhere, not only in Japan but also in America and England. But then there were no Japanese cars. The few we saw on the streets of Yokohama had been made, years before, in America or England. Our car was American.

Getting in, I found myself sitting by a window with no glass in it. It was still raining, and I had no shelter from the rain. But at least we were moving, on the way to our new home.

Once we were out of Yokohama, I could feel I was at last in Japan. The city had been so Western in appearance, though in need of repair. But the countryside was Eastern, as it had always been. Here was the old, the real Japan, where the Japanese were really themselves, I thought.

It was raining all the time, and there was thick mist everywhere. It seemed to me that the mist was part of the countryside. It was (I felt) what had made Japan. It must have entered into the minds and hearts of the Japanese from the dawn of their history. It rose all round us, like the ghost of old Japan. It even seemed about to enter into our minds and hearts, too.

The mist not only came down from the clouds: it also rose up from the rice fields. The Japanese almost lived on rice, now in these post-war years more than ever before. They were all little fields, many of them together, but between them people had made banks of earth, and little streams of

The sea-port of Yokohama.

The mist rises from the rice fields.

water. The streams brought water into the fields for the thirsty rice plants. And from all this water, the mist rose up into the air.

There were many houses, too, by the roadside. Almost all of them were poor houses, made of wood, with roofs of tin. In them we could see the poverty of post-war Japan. Here and there we passed an open door. Inside, everything seemed so neat.

Although the Japanese were poor, they were happy enough. They seemed to be busy all the time, with no free time to be lazy. At least they were able to live. They were close to nature in the countryside. And they had many children to comfort them.

As for the children, they seemed to spend all their spare time playing – as children should. They seemed so much happier than the children today, who are fed too much, and forced to study too much. They never seemed to quarrel or cry. Once I noticed a small child falling off his toy bicycle onto the road. Yet instead of crying, he was laughing. It seemed to him a kind of joke, even if it brought him some pain.

Then we came to the mountains. Perhaps in height they were only hills, but to me they looked like mountains. They rose suddenly and sharply from the plain. In England the countryside is usually rolling, never quite flat and rarely steep. But here the plains, with rice fields in them, were perfectly flat. Then, when the mountains began, they rose up steeply into the sky. Their tops were hidden from us in the mist.

"Japan," I was informed by my friends, "is a largely mountainous country. Almost two-thirds of the country is taken up by mountains; only a third is left for the people to live in. So they are crowded together in the plains and the valleys. There are a hundred million of them, living together in an area smaller than England. So they have to be careful not to step on each other's toes."

"Yes," I thought, "but how happy they are to be living so close to the mountains. They may feel like prisoners in the cities, but they can always escape to the mountains from time to time. And there they can feel free."

The sea, too, is always around them. For Japan is, as her people fully realise, an island country. She is, in fact, not one but many islands. We were in the main island of Honshu. But there were also the islands of Hokkaido in the North, Shikoku in the West, and Kyushu in the South, besides little islands without number. I felt a similarity with the British Isles.

"Yes," I said to myself again, "I have travelled halfway across the world, from the West to the East, to Japan. Here, the people and their country are so different from England. But are they really so different? After all, we are both island countries; and that says a lot. I have seen so many differences now. But in time, perhaps I will realise the deeper similarities that unite us as human beings."

That is just what I have found. The differences between the English and the Japanese can be seen by anyone. But the similarities are deep in the heart of man. And for me, both the differences and the similarities are precious.

Chapter Two
The Language of the Islanders

By the time we reached our new home, it had stopped raining. The sun was even kind enough to appear from among the clouds. We got out of the car and looked around us. The Japanese navy used to have a base here, beside a harbour like the one at Yokohama. One of the buildings looked older than the others and in need of a fresh coat of paint. It was to be our new home.

It was also to be our language school. Here we would live for the next two years, and study the Japanese language. I saw it as a kind of prison; we were the prisoners, and the study of Japanese was our form of punishment. Still, it wasn't too bad. At least, it was next to the sea and surrounded by mountains. From time to time, we could leave our work and go for walks up the mountains. There, like the Japanese, we could feel free.

When I say "we", I now mean not only the three of us who had just come by ship all the way from England. There were many others, of different nations, waiting to welcome us at the language school – some thirty students in two years. We had all come to spend our lives in Japan. So we were ready to give up two full years to learn Japanese.

"After all," I said to myself, "what have I seen so far of Japan and the Japanese? Only the surface. I still understand nothing about the land and her people. I am just like a tourist. In order to know the heart of this people, there is only one way; I must learn their language. Then I can speak with them in their own words, and they can speak with me, heart to heart."

Our language school was next to a high school for boys. Term-time had just begun. It was their second term, as in Japan the school year starts in April. The boys were between the ages of twelve and eighteen, and every day we saw them coming along the road to the school or going home. They were always talking, laughing and playing on the way. They seemed so different from the older

Japanese in the harbour area at Yokohama. They were the new Japan.

They also provided us with pleasant surroundings for our study of Japanese. We were much older than them, but in our study of Japanese, we felt no different from them. We seemed to be children again. Here was a completely new language for all of us in the first year. And we were in a new country, surrounded by new people. So we felt gradually renewed in mind and heart.

The first sentence we had to learn in Japanese was '*Kore wa hon desu*' – 'This is a book'. It reminded me of the first sentence I learned in French at the age of seven: 'This is the pen of my aunt.' '*Kore wa*' means 'this'; '*hon*' means 'book'; and '*desu*' means 'is'.

But these two sentences in English and Japanese are by no means the same. What is the '*wa*' doing in the Japanese sentence? And where is the English word 'a'? And why is the order of words different in Japanese, with 'is' at the end?

Here, in my first Japanese sentence, I found three basic differences between English and Japanese. Let me explain them one by one.

In the first place, the Japanese '*wa*' isn't expressed in English. It takes the place of the emphasis we put on words. The Japanese never emphasise their words. So when Japanese students read English, they do so in a flat voice, without any emphasis.

Secondly, the Japanese have no 'a' or 'the', as we have. They hardly notice any difference between one thing and many things. For them the important thing is simply 'thing'. So '*hon*' might be one book or many books; the Japanese sentence doesn't tell us.

That seems very simple, much simpler than the English differences between 'a thing' and 'the thing'; between 'things' and 'the things'. But the Japanese have their own complications when they speak of different kinds of things.

On the whole, however, Japanese grammar is fairly simple. If the only difficulty in Japanese was its grammar, I would be very happy. But we found there are other kinds of difficulty. One of the chief kinds was the huge number of unfamiliar words. We could see no connection between '*hon*' and 'book'. We just had to force the new words into our poor old memories.

Japanese is such a rich language. It never seems to forget or throw away any words it has picked up in the course of time. Some words are used only in writing, never in speaking. So when we read a new word, we didn't know if we could also speak it. We could only ask our Japanese teachers, if they were around.

At the end of our language course, I was speaking in Japanese with a Japanese friend of mine. Suddenly, he began to laugh at me. "Why are you laughing?" I asked him. "What mistake have I made in Japanese?" "You haven't made any mistake," he replied. "Your Japanese is perfect. But we never speak like that." Then I realized that I must unlearn much of what I had learnt so painfully.

That isn't all, however. Japanese has been called one of the most difficult languages in the world. Indeed, at our language school people said that Japanese must have been invented by the devil. He didn't want foreigners like ourselves to speak with the people!

Another difficulty for us was the use of polite or honourable words. And of course there were other words not so polite or honourable. (Though in Japanese there are few swear-words.) The Japanese are such a polite people. I think they are the politest people on earth. And this politeness is echoed in their words.

For example, if a man means 'I', he usually says '*watakushi*', and a woman says '*watashi*'. But with friends, you may say '*boku*', or perhaps '*ore*'. But usually you don't need to mention the 'I' at all.

This may all seem rather confusing. But to me it was very pleasing. It showed me how polite the Japanese were. In any case, a foreigner didn't need to use all these honourable words. It was enough for me to know the common forms of speech, with only a few of the honourable words.

I still have to speak about the most difficult problem of all: writing in Japanese. Instead of the English letters, they have two sets of signs: 'a, i, u, e, o; ka, ki, ku, ke, ko; sa, shi, su, se, so' – and so on. In each set there are some forty-two signs. One set, called *hiragana*, is more flowing and is mostly used for Japanese words. The other set, called *katakana*, is mostly used for foreign words.

And there are the many Chinese signs or *kanji*. Each of these is formed with several strokes of the pen (sometimes as many as thirty strokes). We had to learn about two thousand of these signs in two years. But we had to learn many more as well, even to read the daily newspaper.

Here, it seemed, was an almost impossible job. But, strangely, I found it not impossible but delightful. To me it was a kind of game. I gathered *kanji*, as a small boy might gather birds' eggs. I looked for new *kanji* in reading, or while travelling by train. "The more the better," I said to myself.

At the end of two years, I could express my thoughts somehow in Japanese, even if people laughed. I could also more or less understand other people. But I was still far from perfect in the language, especially in reading and writing. And I still had many words to unlearn, and even more to learn.

I have found that the learning of Japanese is endless. Today, people sometimes ask, "How

These are the two sets of Japanese signs:

HIRAGANA

	A あ	I い	U う	E え	O お
K	ka か	ki き	ku く	ke け	ko こ
S	sa さ	si (shi) し	su す	se せ	so そ
T	ta た	ti (chi) ち	tu (tsu) つ	te て	ro と
N	na な	ni に	nu ぬ	ne ね	no の
H	ha は	hi ひ	hu (fu) ふ	he へ	ho ほ
M	ma ま	mi み	mu む	me め	mo も
Y	ya や		yu ゆ		yo よ
R	ra ら	ri り	ru る	re れ	ro ろ
W	wa わ	(w)i ゐ		(w)e ゑ	(w)o を
	Final N ん				
G	ga が	gi ぎ	gu ぐ	ge げ	go ご
Z	za ざ	zi (ji) じ	zu ず	ze ぜ	zo ぞ
D	da だ	zi (ji) ぢ	zu づ	de で	do ど
B	ba ば	bi び	bu ぶ	be べ	bo ぼ
P	pa ぱ	pi ぴ	pu ぷ	pe ぺ	po ぽ

KATAKANA

	A ア	I イ	U ウ	E エ	O オ
K	ka カ	ki キ	ku ク	ke ケ	ko コ
S	sa サ	si (shi) シ	su ス	se セ	so ソ
T	ta タ	ti (chi) チ	tu (tsu) ツ	te テ	to ト
N	na ナ	ni ニ	nu ヌ	ne ネ	no ノ
H	ha ハ	hi ヒ	hu (fu) フ	he ヘ	ho ホ
M	ma マ	mi ミ	mu ム	me メ	mo モ
Y	ya ヤ		yu ユ		yo ヨ
R	ra ラ	ri リ	ru ル	te レ	ro ロ
W	wa ワ	(w)i ヰ		(w)e ヱ	(w)o ヲ
Final N ン			V ヴ		
G	ga ガ	gi ギ	gu グ	ge ゲ	go ゴ
Z	za ザ	zi (ji) ジ	zu ズ	ze ゼ	zo ゾ
D	da ダ	zi (ji) ヂ	zu ヅ	de デ	do ド
B	ba バ	bi ビ	bu ブ	be ベ	bo ボ
P	pa パ	pi ピ	pu プ	pe ペ	po ポ

long did it take you to learn Japanese?'' I say not ''two years'' but ''thirty years''.

Chapter Three
Up and Down the Islands

Though we felt like prisoners in the language school, we had our days of freedom. Once a week we were allowed a day of rest, in addition to Sunday. Then we could go on walks to explore the surroundings of our school. It was surprising how quickly we could get away from the houses and up the mountains. There we really felt free.

There we could see for ourselves that Japan was not only an island country but also a mountain country. Indeed, we hardly yet thought of Japan as an island country. It seemed to spread out in all directions, so far as we could see. But we could see mountains everywhere. There we could walk for many miles without meeting anyone.

In these walks, I specially noticed the steepness of the mountains. I had noticed it already on our arrival. But now I could experience it more fully. Not only did their slopes rise up steeply to the tops of the mountains, but their tops were sharply pointed. A path usually ran along the top and connected one mountain with another. We could walk for several miles along such paths. It was almost like walking along the edge of a razor. We could look down, perhaps to the sea on one side and to more mountains on the other.

On other days we could go sight-seeing to the nearby city of Kamakura. It was only three stops away on the local railway line. We were attracted to Kamakura by its rich historical past, which is still to be seen in the present. It had once been the capital city of Japan.

Wherever we walked in Kamakura, we came across old temples. They all had a special history of their own. Indeed, history surrounded them like the air. They reminded me of the saying of Confucius: '*By studying the past, we understand the present.*' Here in Kamakura, we had a good chance to study the past history of Japan.

For the modern history of Japan, we had (of course) the great capital city of Tokyo. Its name means 'the Eastern capital'. From time to time, we were able to go up to this capital, about 40 miles away, by train.

The train stopped at many stations on the way to Yokohama. Then it ran almost non-stop, for thirty minutes, to Tokyo. On this stretch of line, many small houses, more like huts, reached out in all directions. I hardly saw any large houses or buildings. The only large buildings we passed in the train were school buildings. In the post-war rebuilding of Japan, education seemed to come first. "And rightly so," I thought.

Since that time, over the past thirty years, I have seen with my own eyes the rebuilding of Japan. Whenever I came up to Tokyo, I saw new buildings going up. They didn't take ages to complete, as often happens in England. They were completed like magic, in a moment. When one was finished, another was begun. Or rather, many were built at the same time.

When I saw this great city of Tokyo as a city of huts, I remembered the war, not so long before. Then the whole city had been destroyed by American bombs, even more thoroughly than Hiroshima. None of them had been atomic bombs. But many fire-bombs had been just as effective.

Only in the centre of Tokyo had large buildings survived the bombing. Some were banks; some were theatres; some were department stores. Many of the department stores were along the Ginza, the famous shopping street of Tokyo. They were proof that Japan wasn't such a poor country after all. At least, by then Japan was already well on her way to recovery.

The streets of Tokyo, even the Ginza, were by no means well made. Or perhaps they had once been well made. But now – like everything else in Japan – they were very much in need of repair. The chief means of public transport were the street-cars, the buses and one underground railway-line. The street-cars ran on rails in the middle of the road. The buses had to run between the rails and the pavement. The underground railway chiefly ran underneath the Ginza; and so it was called the Ginza Line.

As for the taxis, it was safer not to use them, if you prized your life. Every taxi-driver seemed to drive as fast as possible, and to take as many risks as possible. They were commonly called by the name of those pilots who offered their lives in the war: *kamikaze*.

The summer after our arrival, we went on our first journey to the Fuji area. I don't say Mount Fuji, since the area was much larger than I expected. From Tokyo Bay in the distance, it had seemed small enough, just one among many mountains. But now the more we approached it, the more it seemed to hide itself. It was famous for being shy of foreign visitors, like the Japanese themselves.

That time, we could still see the mountain only from a distance. But it looked so beautiful, on the far side of a lake, in between the trees. "Perhaps," I said to myself, "this holy mountain is best seen from a distance. It is best seen among trees in blossom, or mountain lakes."

The next time, however, not only did we go close, but we climbed to the top of the mountain. We were a group of six or seven, and we had allowed two days for the climb. We went up during the night, when it was cool. It must have taken us at least six hours. Our aim was to reach the top in time for the sunrise.

Then, while we were climbing, I realised the

mountain was nothing but a great pile of ashes. It was only a sleeping volcano. Close up, it lost all its beauty, and all its romance. It became only a challenge to mountain climbers like ourselves. And we were not the only ones to take up the challenge. We were just part of a long procession climbing upwards to the top.

Still, when we reached the top, our hard climb was richly rewarded. Never in my life had I really seen a sunrise. I mean, I had never watched a sunrise in all its stages. It is more than just the rising of the sun. It begins with the first faint signs of dawn in the eastern sky, and ends with the coming of the sun himself in all his glory. It was a sight to be ever remembered.

It was the most exciting moment of my stay in Japan. On my arrival I had seen Mount Fuji in the distance, in the weak light of sunset. But now, from the top of Fuji, I was able to see this glorious sunrise. Then I remembered the name of Japan, 'the land of the rising sun'.

Chapter Four
Memories of the Islanders

For our study of Japanese at the language school, we used an interesting textbook. We called it '*Naganuma*' from the name of its author. It introduced us not only to the language, but also to the history and folk tales of Japan. It made the language itself more interesting.

So much of old Japan, especially in the cities, had been destroyed in the war. Yet much still remained, especially in the countryside. It was Mr Naganuma who showed us this old Japan. We imagined him as a dear old man. The new post-war Japan was only beginning to appear, and to take the place of the old.

It was natural for us to begin our study of old Japan with Kamakura. We could visit it as often as we liked, and we could see its historical spots with our own eyes. Fortunately, it had escaped destruction during the war. It was full of history, and of religion.

As an ancient capital of Japan, the history of Kamakura went back to the twelfth century. It was then that a family called Genji came to power in the land. They had won a great victory over the rival family. The leaders were two brothers; the hero was the younger brother. He was the brave warrior, and everyone loved him. But his elder brother, Yoritomo, was the political leader. Gradually he became jealous of his popular brother and drove him to his death.

So it was Yoritomo who set up the capital at Kamakura, and so began 'the Kamakura period'.

Another historical city within easy reach of Tokyo was Nikko. We met it in one of the early chapters of Naganuma. Later on, we were able to see it for ourselves. There we learned a famous saying in Japanese: "Until you have seen Nikko, you can't speak of beauty."

The city was specially famous for its fine temples. But they weren't so old as the temples at

Kamakura. And they were rather too brightly painted for the Japanese taste. Here was the chosen place of another great military leader of Japan, Ieyasu; his family of Tokugawa ruled Japan from 1600 to the mid-nineteenth century. And here he lies buried.

As for myself, I preferred the beauty of a lake in the mountains above Nikko, Lake Chuzenji. Whenever we went to Nikko, we would first visit the gaily coloured temples. Then we continued up the steep mountain road to Lake Chuzenji. "Here," I said to myself, "is real beauty. Here I can feel the freedom of nature."

A temple at Nikko

Lake Chuzenji

It was the Tokugawa rulers who first made Tokyo the capital city of Japan. The name was only changed to Tokyo, 'the Eastern capital', in the nineteenth century. It was a sign of the end of Tokugawa rule, and of Japan's looking to the West.

All this time, the true capital of Japan was the town that housed the head of state – the emperor. And that was neither at Kamakura nor at Tokyo (in the East), but at Kyoto (in the West). Here the emperor had lived since the end of the eighth century. Here he was recognized as head of state even when the country was ruled by generals, called *shogun*, such as Yoritomo and Ieyasu.

So Kyoto was far richer in historical memories than either Tokyo or Kamakura. It was also far richer in temples and other ancient buildings. It was some time before I could visit Kyoto. But when I went there at last, I was attracted less by the temples than by their gardens. In the gardens, I could feel something of the beauty and the freedom of nature.

"The Japanese," I again said to myself, "are indeed a nation of gardeners. There are no gardens in the world to compare with Japanese gardens. They are so lovely, so delicate."

The gardens at Kyoto.

The memories of Kyoto centred on the time before the Kamakura period. In fact, almost everything that is really Japanese seems to go back to this time.

Yet not far from Kyoto, there is the even older capital of Nara. Here was the centre of the Nara period during the eighth century. Even today it is full of memories, especially religious memories, from that time. Here we could see many great temples, including one with a huge statue of the Buddha.

In between Tokyo and Kyoto, the Eastern and the old capital, there runs the historical road called the Tokaido. It means 'the way of the Eastern Sea', because it follows the coastal plain near the Eastern Sea – what we call the Pacific Ocean. It was chiefly used during the Tukogawa period.

There were then two main commercial centres in Japan: Tokyo in the East, and Osaka – not Kyoto – in the West. In this period, commerce was more important than ever before; the middle class rose to importance in the life of the nation.

The new middle class lived very differently from the ruling class of warriors, or 'samurai'. The warriors followed a simple, plain way of life. But the merchants were more easy-going in their

The Todaiji Temple and statue of Buddha at Nara.

ways, and they combined profit with pleasure.

"But," you may ask, "what about Japan's relations with the West?" That was a matter of deep interest to us all. For we had all come from the West, and we expected to spend the rest of our lives in Japan.

The West's first introduction to Japan was on the southern island of Kyushu. Here the first Portuguese sailors had come to Japan about the mid-sixteenth century. And soon after them came the first Christian missionary, St. Francis Xavier. It was from this time onwards that Christianity began to spread in Japan, with its centre in Nagasaki. In fact, this period, the second half of the sixteenth century, is sometimes called the *Kirishitan*, or Christian, period.

For a time, the Christians were helped by the local rulers. But then the country came under the power of a single ruler. The new rulers drove the foreign missionaries from the country. Then they forced the Japanese Christians to give up their new religion. They decided to shut out all Western influence. So they began the policy of *Sakoku*, or closing the country.

This decision remained unchanged for more than three centuries, during the Tokugawa period. But it came to an end with the arrival of the 'black ships' under the American naval commander, Commodore Perry. He forced the Japanese to do business with his country. The

English and the French were not slow to follow his example.

This led to the end of the Tokugawa rulers, and the emperor came back to power in 1868. He moved from the old capital to Tokyo. Under his rule, Japan opened up to the West. But she also did her best to rival the European nations in everything modern. There was a sudden change in the country from the old to the new, from the past to the present. But it was too sudden.

From now on, the Japanese followed the German example for their army, as well as in law and medicine; and the English example for their navy, as well as in politics and manners. Then with a modern army and navy, they began to make war on other nations. First, against Russia in the early years of this century. Then against China in the 'thirties. And against England and America in World War Two.

But, their early victories against Russia and China had given the Japanese too much confidence. So when they joined in the Second World War, they went too far. The result was the sad destruction of most of their cities, as we ourselves had seen in Yokohama and Tokyo. Now they had to begin all over again, almost from nothing.

Chapter Five
Something Strange about the Islands

From the time of my arrival in Yokohama, I had felt something strange about my new island home. The feeling came to me in the thick mist on that first ride in the American car. Yes, it had been strange; the mist had seemed to swallow up everything in the countryside.

Then there was that old naval base among the hills. While we were there, we were invaded by insects. They were not the small insects we have in England, but large ones of every kind. And there were so many of them! "Indeed," I said to myself, adding one more item to the growing list, "Japan is a land of insects!"

Then there was the Japanese language we had to learn with so much pain. There was something strange in the words, especially (I thought) the written words. The characters didn't even have their origin in Japan: they had come from China. I took delight in learning them. But I was also partly afraid of them. With all their delicate strokes, they were strange.

Our Japanese teacher lived in the nearby city of Zushi and he told us many ghost stories. In Zushi, he said, there were many ghosts, and many more ghost stories. I asked him if he had ever seen a ghost. "No," he answered, "but I've heard of so many." It was the usual answer to such a question.

When we arrived, the season for ghost stories had just come to an end. In Japan, the common time for telling such stories isn't winter – as it is in England – but summer, in the month of August. The reason is simple and practical. In summer it is hot, and ghost stories can make you feel cool, without the need of ice!

Most of the ghosts I heard about were women. Was it because women are more mysterious than men? I don't really know. But not many of the ghosts had been human beings. Most of them were strange monsters, dwelling in special places. They all had one thing in common: they were all without legs!

When I visited the old temples in Kamakura, it was easy to believe these ghost stories. The temples themselves were like ghosts of old Japan. They were always built of wood, and the wood was usually old and rotten. They were also badly in need of repair. And they were surrounded by the graves of the dead.

Once I met a group of high-school girls who were staying a few days at one of these temples. "Do you like staying here?" I asked them. "No," they replied. "But why?" I asked again. "Don't you find it peaceful here?" "It's too peaceful," was their answer. "And we're afraid of seeing ghosts among the graves."

Still, this isn't quite what I mean by the strangeness of Japan. There are many ghost stories in this country. But there are just as many in England. Even more than Japan, England may well be called a land of ghosts!

The feeling came to me again when I visited the area round Mount Fuji. As I have said, Fuji is a sleeping volcano. But the whole area is volcanic. And it isn't always sleeping either. Wherever you go, clouds of steam are rising up from the earth. You hear a strong 'ssssss', and you may be afraid till you realise what it is.

Among the hills at the foot of Mount Fuji, I came across a strange valley. It was bare earth and rock. Hardly any plants could grow there. Down the valley came a stream of hot, dirty-looking water. On either side, clouds of steam burst into the air from the red rock. It was like a scene in hell!

But almost everywhere in Japan seems to be volcanic. The islands seem to be resting on a large sleeping volcano, and it may awake at any moment. Yet the islanders themselves don't worry. They are happy to use all this hot water for baths. Round the hot springs, they build special hotels called *onsen*. Here, too, they can combine profit with pleasure.

As for Mount Fuji herself, she is indeed a magic mountain. But you have to look at her from a distance. There is magic in her form, her shape, her slopes. But the magic disappears when you go too close.

My eyes and ears told me this within the first year of my stay in Japan. At that time, it was still the old Japan. And in that old Japan, it was easy to go still further back into the past – the past that I found in the pages of Naganuma. I could go back and back – into the Tokugawa period, the Kirishitan period, the Kamakura period, till I became lost in the mists of the past.

But the mystery wasn't just in the past. Nor was it just in the land, nor just in its memories, nor just in its stories about ghosts and monsters. It was rather, I thought, in the living people I met.

There was a mystery in their faces. There was a mystery in their silence; I had noticed it in the workers in the harbour area at Yokohama. There was a mystery in their smiling, and even their laughing; I had noticed it in the child as he fell off his toy bicycle. There was a mystery even in their talking and playing; I had noticed it in the schoolboys on their way to school in the morning.

This was the mystery I felt around me everywhere, especially during those two years at the language school. It was a mystery similar to the sunrise, as I watched it from the top of Mount Fuji. At first, all was dark, with only the stars above. Then the first signs of light appeared in the

East, with the dance of the morning star. And then they turned into bright rays of sunlight shooting up into the sky.

At last, the sun rose and it was day. So, after two years of patient study, I found I could talk with Japanese people in their own language. What a delight it was for me! I remember a conversation with a Buddhist monk. It was in the depths of winter, and there was snow on the ground. I was passing by a temple, when I noticed the statue of a man. I wanted to know who it was. So I called at the temple and put my question to a monk. He easily answered it. Then we talked of other matters, one after another. Before I realised it, we had been talking for two hours, in Japanese. And all the time I had been standing at the entrance, in the cold.

So the mystery had a simple answer. Everything in Japan had seemed strange, because I myself was the stranger. Everything had seemed strange, because I couldn't yet speak with the people. But once I learned the language, my feeling of strangeness disappeared. Or rather the mystery of Japan changed for me into the mystery of man.

Chapter Six
Customs of the Islanders

I wasn't long in Japan before I began to notice certain typical ways of behaving among the Japanese. What was natural to the Japanese was strange to me.

The Japanese are such a polite people. They bend their bodies forward before they say anything. One of the first things I noticed was this habit of bowing.

When two friends meet in the street, especially if they are old women, they first bow to each other. They don't just bow once; they have to bow many times. While bowing to each other, they are usually saying something. But what they are saying isn't important. It's just a fixed form of greeting. There are many fixed forms of this kind, for use at different times. Most are expressions of politeness, with no special meaning.

I noticed this politeness in the bus-girls, who sold us our tickets on the buses. They were always thanking everyone for the smallest reason. At the end of our journey, they stood at the door and took our tickets with a low bow and a word of thanks. They said, "Each time you take our bus, thank you very much!"

Even the boys at the nearby high-school were

polite. They knew that we were from the language school. So whenever they passed us on the road, they took off their caps and bowed.

And they were so obedient. I wouldn't have believed it, if I hadn't seen it with my own eyes. There they were talking and laughing in front of the school building. Then the bell rang for classes to begin. At once they all stood still like statues, till the ringing came to an end. Then they all ran – not walked, but ran – to their different classrooms.

Inside the classrooms (I was told) it was the same. They stood beside their desks, and waited for the teacher to arrive. When he came in, he bowed to them and they bowed to him. Only when he said, "You may sit down", did they sit down and open their desks. At least, that was how they behaved in those days. Since then, I hear they have become more human and freer in their ways; but they are less polite and less obedient.

The origin of all this politeness was the Japanese home. Here, at the very entrance, I had to take off my shoes before going in. When I first had to do this, I had the feeling of stepping on holy ground. It is a sign that you honour the people inside. This must have a deep effect on everything one does and feels inside the house.

At the entrance, there were soft, loose shoes. You put these slippers on before you walked on the wooden floor outside the rooms. But when you entered a room, you had to take off the slippers too. It was forbidden to walk on the rice-mats, or *tatami*, with any kind of shoes. If the house was holy, the rooms of the house were even holier.

In the middle of the room there was a low table, and there were cushions on the floor round the table. The proper way of sitting was to bend your knees forward and sit back on your feet. But I was never able to keep this position for long. It was so painful. My Japanese friends kindly allowed me to take a more comfortable position. But my difference from the others in the room made me feel more uncomfortable. Although I was among friends, I was still a stranger.

There was one corner of the room which was especially holy. It was called the *tokonoma*. In it, there was a bowl of flowers beautifully arranged in the Japanese way. Behind the bowl, on the wall, there was a long painting of mountains and rivers; it might be of birds and flowers. These, I had learned in Naganuma, are the fixed forms of Japanese painting from the past. I wanted to sit on a cushion facing this lovely corner. But as the honoured guest I had to sit with my back to it.

There are all kinds of customs in Japanese life, which I will never get to know, especially in the countryside. I have been in Japan now for thirty years, but I have hardly begun to know them. All this time, of course, the customs themselves have been gradually disappearing, and a new, Westernised Japan has appeared. In one way, I feel sad about their disappearance. But in another way, it makes life easier and simpler for me – and for the Japanese, too.

There still remains one area of life, however, where the power of custom is as strong as ever: the area of marriage. Although post-war Japan has become increasingly Westernised, few marriages are based on love. Many are still arranged by the parents, though the children still have the right to say "No!". When the children *do* make their own choice, the parents have the right to say "No!" if they don't approve.

When the couple have at last decided to go

ahead with the marriage, their path is still not easy. They then begin to feel the full weight of Japanese custom. There are so many people for them to visit; relations have to be told about the marriage, in person. There are so many journeys to be made, so many gifts to be presented, so many nice words to be spoken. There is an exchange of presents between the couple and their families. There are also preparations to be made for the wedding itself, and for the feast after the wedding. The wedding feast is the high point of Japanese custom. Other things in Japanese life have been Westernised, but on this point the Japanese have kept their customs of marriage unchanged.

I have had wide experience, as a university teacher, of Japanese weddings. And as a Westerner, I have to admit that they are mostly very painful. The people are so polite, so fixed in their ways, so deeply rooted in Japanese custom. The poor couple can never feel at ease from beginning to end. The feast is as much of a religious act as the wedding itself. At events like this I feel I have moved back into history.

Yes, politeness is a good thing. It is something I admire in the Japanese. But it isn't always so good. It is possible to carry a good thing too far. Even the Japanese themselves admit it. They would like to break out of the chains of social custom. But the chains are too strong. After all, man is a creature of custom. On this point, the Japanese are very human. If they give up the old customs, will the new customs be any better?

So I don't want the Japanese to give up all their old customs. I don't want them to take over the free and easy customs of the West. I want them to be polite, as they've always been, but not too polite. I want them to keep their customs, but within reasonable limits. But where are the limits? That isn't such an easy question to answer.

Chapter Seven
What They Eat

I've already mentioned the table in a Japanese house. But I didn't say what was on the table. When an honoured guest arrives, the table is unlikely to be empty. Or if it is empty, it won't be empty for long.

Even if you are only visiting for a minute or two, the minutes soon become fifteen, and sometimes thirty. Shortly after you enter the guest-room, the wife of the house quietly enters with some Japanese tea. With the tea there is usually a Japanese tea-cake, made of crushed beans. But the wife rarely remains. She usually departs as quietly as she entered.

The Japanese are proud of their food. When a foreigner comes to Japan, he is soon asked, "What do you think of the country?" But then he is asked, not about Japanese art, or the Japanese language, or the countryside of Japan, "How do you like our food?" they ask him eagerly. If he is polite, he will say, "I like it very much, thank you." Sometimes, as in my case, he will also mean it.

In England, we rarely ask foreigners' opinions of our English food. We're not ashamed of it, of course. For me, it's still some of the best food in the world. But we think it is bad manners to ask such a question of our guests. In Japan, however, it's a mark of politeness to put this all-important question.

"Well, then," you may ask, "what is Japanese food and Japanese cooking like?" Well, I answer, to begin with, it's very special. You mustn't think of it as a form of Chinese cooking. The Chinese cook for the stomach, and for the tongue, but the Japanese prepare food for the eye. They don't completely forget the tongue or the stomach, but what they chiefly regard is the eye. It is part of their general concern for appearances.

Every Japanese dish is indeed a work of art. It is laid out so neatly, so pleasingly to the eye. I feel it is a shame to disturb the order. I would almost prefer to go without the food; then I could go on enjoying the sight of it.

Variety is one of the main qualities of food in Japan. In England, we are quite satisfied with a few favourite dishes. But the Japanese are never satisfied. They are always exploring, always looking out for new dishes. They seem willing to eat anything.

"Surely," you may object, "they won't eat poison." Yes, I answer, they will and they do. Near their shores there is a kind of fish called 'blow-fish' or *fugu*. Parts of this fish are very poisonous. Yet the Japanese are so fond of it, they will still eat it. They may die afterwards. One famous Japanese actor did die, quite recently, after he ate *fugu*. But there are others who obey the common saying: "I like *fugu*, but I prefer my life."

The Japanese have always been fond of fish for their table. But recently, as a result of American influence, they have begun to eat meat. When the 'black ships' first arrived, the Americans taught the Japanese to eat meat and drink milk. You can still see a memorial to the American who taught them these things, in a city called Shimoda.

You can see a wide variety of fish in Japanese shops and on Japanese tables. In one meal alone,

I counted over fifteen different kinds of fish. At this meal my Japanese host took delight in telling me the names of all the fishes, and where and when they were usually caught. I was so surprised. In England, we only have three or four kinds of fish. And few people know or care very much about where or when they are caught. "Surely," we think, "such fish are caught anywhere in the sea at any time of the year."

There is another thing that is even more surprising to foreign visitors. Instead of boiling the fish, or frying it, as we do in England, the Japanese like to eat it raw. Of course, they do sometimes boil or fry their fish, but they prefer it raw. They cut it up in small pieces and lay it out on green leaves. It is laid out so simply and neatly. It is so artistic. The colour pattern is so beautiful. I hardly feel like eating it.

"But what's it like to eat?" you may ask again. Of course, you don't take it straight from the dish and put it into your mouth. That would be rude. No, there is something important in between. There is a small saucer of liquid – soy-sauce. The Japanese take soy-sauce with almost everything they eat, especially raw fish. And into the soy-sauce, they put a strong kind of pepper called *wasabi*.

But you mustn't do what I did the first time I had a Japanese meal with raw fish. Beside the fish I noticed some nice-looking green stuff. So I thought I'd try that first. Before anyone could stop me, I put it all into my mouth. It didn't remain there for long. But while it was there, it burnt like the fires of hell. It seemed to be making a hole in my tongue. I won't easily forget it. As we say, "The burnt cat fears the fire."

There is another common way of cooking fish and vegetables. The Japanese call it *tempura*. It was brought to Japan by the Portuguese missionaries in the sixteenth century. But now the Japanese think of it as their own way of cooking. They are even surprised to hear that it ever came from abroad. If it came from anywhere, they think, it must have come from heaven. In writing it, they begin with the Chinese sign for 'heaven'.

This isn't raw fish, but a way of frying fish and vegetables. It is very tasty, while it is hot. But it soon gets cold, if you forget to eat it before anything else. It is commonly served with raw fish. Then, of course, you have to eat it before the raw fish.

Together with the fish and various vegetables, there is always rice. For the Japanese, bread is characteristic of the West. As for potatoes, they are only one among many vegetables to go with the rice. They always serve rice in a special bowl. You are supposed to eat all other kinds of food with a mouthful of rice.

Further, the Japanese prepare rice differently from the English. In England, when we have rice with chicken, it is often rather hard, or else soft and dry. But in Japan, however, it is soft and wet and sticky. So it easily sticks together; and it is easily picked up with chopsticks.

Here I must say a word about chopsticks, which are regularly used for eating Japanese food. It is one thing the Japanese have in common with the Chinese. At first, I was awkward with them. Everyone is. But in a short time I got used to them. I even enjoyed moving them up and down. When I used them to put food in my mouth, I thought of a mother bird feeding her young.

But while speaking of food, I must say something of drink as well. After all, you can't eat without drinking something, "to help the food down".

I've already mentioned Japanese tea, which is offered at all times of the day and night. It is usually green, but it may also be light brown. There are perhaps as many kinds of tea in Japan as wines in Europe. To me, however, they all taste more or less alike. I don't mind tea, but my sense of taste isn't so delicate as that of the Japanese.

Then there is the rice-wine known as *sake*. This is poured hot into very small cups. You have to drink it all at once, and then hand out your cup for more. You shouldn't pour it for yourself; that would be rude. But someone else, especially a woman, may pour it for you. It is often taken with raw fish, before the rice is served.

Again, there are many kinds of *sake*, but again, they all taste more or less the same to me. Still, I like them all, so long as they are hot. When they get cold, like *tempura*, they lose their taste. Or if they still have a taste, it is like soap. With a Japanese meal, I usually drink *sake*. But with the spread of Western customs, more Japanese are drinking beer instead of *sake*. Sometimes at a Japanese meal I am the only person drinking *sake*; all the others are drinking beer!

Such is the influence of the West on old Japanese customs, even in the matter of food. Today the Japanese are eating less fish and more meat; less rice and more bread.

Chapter Eight
What They Think

I have been living here in Tokyo for more than twenty years. All this time I have been surrounded by crowds of people. People, people everywhere. When I see them in the streets, or packed together in the trains, I often wonder what they are thinking. I wonder if they are thinking anything. Perhaps they are just being patient. They have to spend so much of their lives being patient.

It seems to me, after thirty years in this country, that the Japanese can't be called 'a nation of thinkers'. From time to time they have to think, when they are forced to do so. But it takes time. And before they say anything, they need to compare their thoughts with those of others. They prefer to express their thoughts in silence rather than in words; they express themselves through what they *don't* do rather than what they do.

This is perhaps why they puzzle Westerners so much, especially in business and politics. They are usually so slow to give an answer. They may seem to be wise and cautious about making a decision. But I sometimes wonder if they are thinking at all. They need time to think over the matter. And, of course, they want to ask the opinion of the experts, who are not usually the top men.

To explain their way of thinking, I would like to follow the advice of Confucius: '*By studying the past, we understand the present.*' I think we can understand the present mind of the Japanese by studying their past religion.

Shinto, or 'the way of the gods', is the oldest religion in Japan. It has many gods, and many strange stories about them. But today almost nobody believes in Shinto. In any case, in Shinto people aren't expected to believe anything. It is rather a religion of customs. It seems to suit the Japanese character; and it still survives.

In the case of Shinto, we speak of 'shrines', rather than temples. Many a time I have watched Japanese, of all ages, coming up to the shrine. First, they throw some money into a large open box there. Then, they clap their hands and join them together in silence. It is only for a moment. That is all.

What are they thinking during that moment? Are they thinking of anything at all? I am too shy to ask them the question. But perhaps they would be surprised if I asked them. "Are you talking silently to your god? Are you praying to him? Do you really believe in him?" "No, not really," they would say. "But it is our custom to pray like that at the shrine. If there is a god, he may hear and answer our prayer."

Yes, I think they would answer like that. In Shinto, they tell strange stories of 'ten thousand gods'. But nobody really believes in them. Instead, they feel something special on mountains like Mount Fuji, in ancient rocks and trees, and even in human beings like the emperor. But it is only a feeling, not a clear thought or belief.

I also find something of this feeling in Buddhism, which came to Japan from China in the seventh century. Buddhism is a very different kind of religion from Shinto. Perhaps it is not really a religion at all, as it has no clear belief in God or gods. But in Japan it has grown together with Shinto over the ages.

These two religions between them have taken over two main areas of human life. Shinto is the religion for life and marriage, while Buddhism is the religion for death. Yet at a Buddhist temple, Japanese pray in the same manner as at a Shinto shrine.

But in Buddhism, there is much more silent prayer than in Shinto. Believers will spend long hours in such silent prayer. There they sit, with a look of perfect peace on their faces. They sit without moving, like statues of the Buddha. And what are they thinking all this time? They aren't supposed to be thinking – at least, they are supposed to be thinking of 'nothing'.

To the Western mind, this way of thinking seems very strange. When we think, we like to think of something. I don't mean that Japanese can't be Christians. But in Christianity, belief in the word of God is of central importance, while Shinto and Buddhism are religions of silence. They have no need of belief.

Chapter Nine
What Interests Them

As a university teacher, I know more about university students than about other Japanese. Suppose, then, you ask me, "What is the main interest of Japanese students today?", what will I answer? I would have to say "sport". I suppose it is much the same in most countries today, including America and England. But it is even more so in Japan. In this country, there are sports newspapers of every kind. They show how popular sports are in Japan. And in the university, half the student clubs are sports clubs.

Then you may ask me again, "Which sport is the most popular among Japanese students?" Their interest is entirely taken up with American baseball. All Japanese boys, and not a few Japanese girls, are keen baseball fans. During a large part of their summer months, they sit glued to their TV sets, watching the baseball games.

Yes, baseball is a sure sign of the American influence on modern Japan. Still, it hasn't completely pushed out the older sports of Japan. At least, there remains the popular form of Japanese fighting known as *sumo*. It is a very professional sport. At least, I don't know of any student club for it. But everyone, young and old, delights in watching *sumo* fights on TV.

I also sometimes watch it on TV. There it seems so typically Japanese. Two fat, half-naked men stand on either side of a narrow ring, with the referee in the middle. He looks just like a Shinto priest. Before the fight begins, the two men have to throw a lot of salt on the ground, for good luck, I suppose. Then at last they can begin. It is the aim of each to push the other out of the ring. Often the fight is over within a few seconds. Then another pair come forward, and it all begins again.

If *sumo* is Shinto in origin, there are other sports that have grown up under Buddhist influence. Such are the Japanese fighting arts of *judo* and *karate*. They both depend not only on skill with hands and feet, but also on concentration of mind. For this they follow the Buddhist way of prayer. They begin with exercises for the mind, to concentrate the powers of the mind. But the object of this concentration isn't the enemy; it is rather oneself. When one has reached this point of concentration, one is ready for anything. No move of the enemy can take one by surprise.

For such sports there are many student clubs. *Sumo* may need a long training. And *sumo* champions have to be fat, much fatter than most university students and most Japanese. But these other sports have a practical use in defending oneself. They also have an interest of their own.

Sumo fighting.

From time to time, the students in these clubs show their skill in public.

I can't speak of all the sports that interest the students; there are so many of them. At least, I must mention tennis, which is now very fashionable among women. There are also table-tennis, swimming, skiing in the mountains, walking, cycling and mountain-climbing.

Next to sports comes music, music of every kind. It is surprising how fond the Japanese are of music; and it is mainly Western music. There are, of course, various kinds of old Japanese music: court music, which sounds strange to Western ears, and music of a more popular nature. I rather like the *koto*, or Japanese harp. It's usually played by women. But nearly all the student clubs are for Western music.

The number of these clubs can hardly be counted. They have bands of all kinds: brass bands, jazz bands and others. There are clubs for different kinds of singing, as well. Of course, rock music is very popular; and the Beatles are still great heroes. Each club arranges its own concerts, usually in public halls.

There is a famous man in this country, called Mr Suzuki. He has developed a way of teaching the violin to small children, even from the age of two or three. His method is now well known all over the world, as the Suzuki method. It works not only with Japanese but also with American

Women playing the koto.

and English children. For children are much the same the world over.

There are so many other clubs, I can't mention them all. Still, there is one I can't leave out. It shows the great interest of young Japanese today in amusing little drawings, called *manga*. This is, of course, the *manga* club. All university students read the popular *manga* magazines. But in the club they try to imitate and improve on the *manga*. I myself, as a teacher, encourage them to add *manga* to the writing they do for me.

Now at last I must turn from clubs to classes. Here again, "What about their classes?" you may ask me. "Aren't the Japanese students interested in their classes?"

Well, among students, the clubs come first, and classes come only second or third. In their clubs, they take a keen pleasure, but their classes are an unpleasant duty. And in modern Japan, especially among students, pleasure comes before duty.

Naturally, there are different kinds of study. When it is practical, as in the case of science and engineering, it may well catch their interest. The Japanese are a practical nation. Or it may be closely connected with their future job. And then they take a professional interest in it. But when it is such a useless subject as English novels, plays or poems, it isn't so attractive. In modern Japan, the study of English is a means of getting a good job.

Lastly, I must turn from the present to the future interests of students. "What are their aims in life?" you may ask.

Well, I answer, I have never met a student who wanted to become a politician. Their desires are more practical and more simple. The boys usually want a good job in a well-known company. The girls want to be good wives and good mothers. And those, I think, are very good and very human aims.

Chapter Ten
What Occupies Them

Now I must try and answer the question that everyone today is asking about the Japanese. "What are they doing on their islands?" people ask. "How do they produce the endless stream of articles that are 'made in Japan'? What is the secret behind all their energy? What is the meaning of all those names that have suddenly become familiar in the Western world: names like Sony and Sanyo, Toyota and Nissan, Hitachi and Honda?"

I've been in Japan for thirty years. I've seen with my own eyes the impossible become possible, and then actual. Thirty years ago it seemed impossible that Japan would ever again become a leading nation in the world. Then they were satisfied just to survive. But today it is not only possible: it is a fact that Japan is a leading nation.

All the same, Japan's recovery remains a mystery to me. The questions that puzzle people about the Japanese today are also a puzzle to me. Indeed, they are more of a puzzle to me. People in the West only see the stream of articles that come from Japan. But I see the Japanese who make the articles. And they are a puzzle to me.

In the minds of Westerners, the Japanese have to be busy all the time, to make so many articles of so many kinds. I agree with them. "But," I ask myself, "are the Japanese busy all the time, as a matter of fact? Have I ever seen them busy all the time?" To be honest, I have to say "No!"

This is the problem, as I see it. It is a problem not of Japanese goods, but of the Japanese character. I can't honestly say that the Japanese are a busy or hard-working nation. Some of them are busy, and some of them work hard. But all of them? No!

Certainly, they seem to be busy, as they hurry along the streets during the rush hour. They seem to be busy, if you look at the number of trains and buses and their passengers. They seem to be busy, if you think of their long hours of work. But are they really busy? No, I don't think so.

I realise, of course, that I'm teaching at a university. And in Japan the university is seen as a place of peace and freedom, in between periods of care and business. Before, they are busy at high-school, preparing for their university exams. They call this time 'examination hell'. After, they are busy with company affairs. So I see them when they are least busy, and most lazy. They even like it when I tell them – half joking, half seriously – that they are lazy. Perhaps they don't believe me; they don't take me seriously at all.

Yet I do meet other Japanese apart from students. I sometimes see them at work in their offices. I see them sitting at their desks, all open to view, in a wide room. There I can see many of them at once. But there they don't seem to be so busy. Many of them seem to have nothing special to do. Only a few of them are really active.

"Here is the reason," I say to myself, "why there is so little unemployment in Japan. Because they don't need to be busy, they can all be employed."

So, the post-war recovery of Japan is a mystery to me. On the other hand, even my lazy students have certain qualities that may explain the mystery.

First, the Japanese are a very ambitious nation. They have even raised a statue in memory of the American, Dr William Clark, who told his students: "Boys, be ambitious!" They have forgotten everything else about Dr Clark. All they remember are these three words of his. And they do their best to follow his advice.

Secondly, in all my students, even the lazy

ones, I find a great energy. This may not appear so much in their studies, least of all in their study of English writers. But it appears in almost everything else, especially in their club activities. After all, their studies, especially of English fiction, are too far from real life. So it is natural for them to be lazy in their studies, and busy in everything else.

Thirdly, they are very practical. They are affected by what they see with their eyes and touch with their hands. For them, such studies as science, engineering and law have an obvious place in modern society. They are practical forms of study. But novels or poems? At best, they might improve one's knowledge of language.

Fourthly, they love making plans. They make plans for everything. They like to arrange everything, in detail. If they go on a journey, they prepare all the details first. When the train departs; when it arrives; how and when to change from one train or bus to another; what to bring with them, and how much to bring. I myself prefer to leave things to chance. But my students want to plan everything. They get so much pleasure out of it.

Fifthly, they like to do things in a group. One by one they may be lazy. They easily find that something is too difficult, and run away from it. But once they are in a group, nothing is too difficult for them.

Sixthly, the Japanese are a patient people. They are ready to put up with every kind of difficulty, so long as they are together. They are in no hurry. They don't mind wasting time. They will put a lot of effort into practising a single action, as in tennis. We Westerners are impatient to get quick results. But the Japanese are perfectly patient. And with their patience, they have got better results than almost any other country in the world.

Lastly, there is their obedience. They are always ready to obey the commands of those above them. Quite often, I notice they are ready to obey before the command is given. Often they hardly wait to understand the command. It is often a blind obedience. Theirs is the spirit that led them to destruction in the war, and now to recovery after the war.

Chapter Eleven
What They Read

"Show me a man's library," we say, "and I'll tell you his character." Well, it really depends how many of his books he has read. Here in Japan, books on a bookshelf don't mean that a person has read them. It only means that he'd like to read them some time. And in many cases that time never comes.

"Well then," you may ask, "what do the Japanese usually read? Not what books do they buy, or keep on their shelves. But what do they actually read?"

I have no doubt about what comes first, at least in the minds of younger Japanese. It is the *manga* magazines and books of funny drawings. The bookshops are full of them. Trains and buses are also full of them. There you may see many students. What are they reading? Not the newspaper, not school books, but these funny books or magazines. Not only on trains and buses, but even in the classroom, many a teacher sees his students reading such books.

There are, of course, other popular magazines as well as the amusing ones. There are weekly magazines of all kinds. Japanese people today seem to prefer magazines to books. And from the magazines they receive a variety of useful, and useless, information. It may be much the same in the West, but I would say it is more so in Japan!

"What then," you may ask, "are the typical subjects of articles in these magazines? What do the Japanese read them for?"

Well, as with student clubs, sport is the most

Manga *drawings from the 15 Days Magazine, 1984.*

popular. There are so many sports magazines, especially for the game of golf.

Then again, as with student clubs, music follows sport. But the weekly magazines emphasise the music-makers rather than the music. I mean the popular singers of the moment, more often female than male. In the past, there have been famous pairs of female singers, such as *The Peanuts* and *The Pink Lady*. But in recent years, singers are more commonly single. Their songs are made popular by TV. But the weekly magazines are more interested in their private lives. And that means their loves and their marriages.

The third place of interest may perhaps be taken by politics. Here again, these magazines are interested, not in politics, but sensation. In recent years, some politicians have made secret deals for money. Such cases make interesting stories for the weekly magazines.

The same is true of business. These magazines aren't interested in business for its own sake. It is rather sensation that attracts them. If you read them, you would hardly guess that Japan was one of the top business nations in the world.

But now, what about books? The Japanese today have certainly not given up reading books. No, indeed.

Up till quite recently there was a flood of books about Japan and the Japanese. Many of these books were written by foreigners and translated into Japanese. They were piled high in almost all the bookshops. The Japanese are very interested in themselves, especially as seen by foreigners.

Other popular books tell the fortunes of their readers by the stars. Almost all Japanese, especially the young, can tell you their star sign. And so they try to learn about their own character. It has nothing to do with religion. Most of them haven't any religion. They are uncertain about the future. But they are afraid that the future may be fixed by fate after all.

Yet other books are those of a practical nature. They are the 'how to' books: how to do this, and how to do that. They are the books that explain things in detail, how to fold paper in various shapes, how to arrange a wedding-feast, how to read and write a book, and so on.

All this time I have been speaking of Japanese writing of today. "But what of their past?" you may ask. "Doesn't it have any influence on the minds of people today?"

Well, their past still lives on; not through what they read on trains or buses, but through what they study in high-school. Here, among other subjects, they have to study Japanese writing. First they have to learn the *kanji*, or Chinese signs, some two or three thousand of them. Till then, they can hardly read or write. Then they can begin to read some of the old writings.

First, I must mention the two great works that have come down to us from the distant past. One is a book of short poems, many of them simple love poems, called the *Manyoshu*. These are all five-line poems, or *tanka*. Each line has a fixed number of sounds, and they are arranged in the pattern: 5-7-5-7-7.

The other work is an early novel, in fact the world's first great novel. It is *The Tale of Genji*. Within a setting of court life in Kyoto, it tells of simple human love and the feelings of men and women.

During the Tokugawa period, the Japanese developed an even shorter kind of poem than those in the *Manyoshu*. This was the *haiku*, with only three lines, and the sounds were arranged in the pattern: 5-7-5. So it is like the *tanka*, but without the ending. The best known *haiku* poet, Matsuo Basho, lived in the seventeenth century. He almost lived for his *haiku*; and wherever he went, he wrote *haiku* about the places he visited. Today these places are marked by stones with the *haiku* written on them. The Japanese don't like to be limited by a fixed subject. They much prefer to be free to write about anything, or everything, or even nothing. They take up their pen, without any special thought in their mind. Then they just write. This way of writing also appears in Japanese novels today.

In these novels, the stories wander here and

there, and their heroes wander with them. Of course, the writers have to speak about a hero and what happens to him. But they are more interested in his thoughts or feelings. He is usually a mask for their own thoughts and feelings.

These novelists have appeared in increasing numbers since the opening of Japan to the West in the mid-nineteenth century. The best known of them, and the best loved, is Soseki Natsume. About the beginning of this century, he spent a few years in London, studying English writing. But on his return home, he gave up his plan of teaching at Tokyo University and became a writer of novels instead. In these novels, he shows the influence of Western customs on the Japan of his day, and his regret at the passing of old Japan. In reading them, I feel deep sympathy for him and for his Japanese readers.

Yet this is the characteristic mood in all Japanese writing: regret for beauty that is passing away. Of course, beauty is passing away all the time. The wonder is that so much still remains, even in modern Japan.

Chapter Twelve
What Entertains Them

What entertains the Japanese? I find the same old order. First comes sport, then music, and then other forms of entertainment. But now I am speaking of professional entertainment.

In sport, of course, baseball comes first. In every city of any size, the largest public place must be for baseball, unless there is an even larger one for athletics. Rock stars give frequent performances in such places.

It is professional baseball which draws the crowds, but there is one form of baseball that is even more popular. It is the high-school baseball which is held every summer in Osaka. During a period of two or three weeks, many thousands of eager people follow the fortunes of their local high-school. These games are given a generous amount of time on TV. Indeed, at this time of the year it is often hard to find anything else on TV.

Next, in matters of music, Tokyo seems to be a kind of centre for the whole world. There are so many excellent concert halls in the city. Musicians, dancers, singers – all the year round they are coming from Europe and America. And if they are at all well known, the hall is sure to be full. In many cases, as when Herbert von Karajan

Korakuen Baseball Stadium in Tokyo.

or Seiji Osawa are conducting, tickets are sold out weeks in advance.

Whenever I go to one of these concert halls, printed advertisements of all kinds are pushed into my hands. They give information about other performances, either at the same place or at other places. Certainly, anyone with any interest in music can easily satisfy his taste to the full. The difficulty is rather to make the best choice among so many possibilities.

Then, from music we may turn to films, which the Japanese prefer to call 'movies'. Again, there is such a variety to choose from in this great capital. All the well-known films, and many others from the West, find their way to Tokyo. In most cases they are more popular than the films made in Japan. So when I ask my students, "What is your hobby?", they often answer, "Watching movies – Western movies."

As for the films made in Japan, there are two really great names I have to mention: the director, Akira Kurosawa, and the actor, Toshiro Mifune. Both are widely known all over the world. And both prefer to direct or act in films with a setting in Japanese history. It is largely thanks to them that there is still a deep interest in old Japan among the younger Japanese. If John Wayne is the typical cowboy for American youth, Mifune is the typical *samurai* (warrior) or *daimyo* (lord) for youth in Japan.

The film industry has suffered from the coming of TV in Japan, as in other countries. Yet for TV viewers there are more chances than ever before to see films. Among the TV films, some kinds are specially popular.

The first presents scenes from modern life, continuing day after day. It usually centres on a problem of love between boy and girl. Viewers are interested because it is so close to their own lives. For foreign students of Japanese, it is an excellent way of learning the language.

Another kind is the *samurai* film, which corresponds in Japan to the 'Wild West' film in America. The hero is always strong and successful. We know he will win in any fight. He may be alone among enemies, but they haven't a chance against him. Such films are often rather poor, but they are still popular.

There is also a series of excellent dramas on Japanese history presented by NHK (the Japanese BBC) on Sunday evenings. They usually last for a whole year. Their subject is often taken from the times of Ieyasu during the late sixteenth century.

Also on NHK, I have to mention the British series of BBC productions of Shakespeare. They give the Japanese a good chance of seeing all the plays of Shakespeare for themselves. They can even choose between the original English, and Japanese translation. The plays of Shakespeare are, of course, presented not only on TV but also on the stage. Only university students (and sometimes high-school students) have the courage to perform them in the original English. Every year I receive many invitations to such performances – more than I can possibly accept. When I can go, I am usually pleased by the acting of the students.

On the professional stage, too, Shakespeare is very popular with Japanese audiences. But for them his plays have to be in Japanese translation. Shakespeare's plays have all been translated into Japanese, not just once but many times. Once I saw a production in a Japanese setting – Shakespeare in Japanese clothes. It was excellent.

Throne of Blood – The Shakespear

I only wish there were others like it. But most Shakespeare productions in Japan follow the Western style.

There are also many public theatres and many professional groups of actors in modern Japan. From time to time they present plays by modern Japanese authors. But it seems that the famous

'ay, Macbeth, in a Japanese setting.

plays of the West have more success. And the most successful are the plays of Shakespeare. Any history of the theatre in modern Japan must give a special place to these performances. They include three tours of Japan made by Britain's Royal Shakespeare Company in the last fifteen years.

"But what about the older Japanese theatre?" you may ask. "Aren't there any plays from old Japan?"

Certainly there are, I answer; and I find them far more interesting than anything on the Japanese stage today. The love of theatre seems to be universal among men. And it has been very well shown by the Japanese from quite early times.

The history of the Noh plays goes back to the Kamakura period. In them the action is slow, the speeches are long, and the setting is simple. There are few actors, usually representing lords and ladies, or gods and ghosts. Today the plays are not so popular, and my students rarely go to them. But they still attract special audiences and foreigners.

The Kabuki plays came later in the Tokugawa period, and they are much more popular. You can feel their popularity in the audience around you. At Noh performances, the audience is polite and silent. But at Kabuki performances they often express their feelings with strange noises. There are more actors on the stage, and their acting

Scenes from Noh Plays.

imitates real life. In the scenery, too, there is more variety and colour. In these plays I feel something of the variety and interest of Shakespeare.

But there are less serious forms of entertainment, which show a Japanese sense of humour. "Is there a Japanese sense of humour?" you may ask in surprise. Well, many Japanese themselves have told me, "We Japanese have no sense of humour." But I can't agree with them. The Japanese theatre does have a sense of humour, a very keen sense of humour. And I can prove it.

First, there is a form of Noh play called *kyogen*. The word means 'silly talk'. The play is a funny performance, to make people laugh. It is added to the more serious plays in a programme of three or four Noh plays. For foreigners, it is usually the most interesting part of the programme.

Secondly, during the Tokugawa period there appeared one-man performances called *rakugo*. These are stories told by a single actor, who remains seated all the time. But they are told in such a lively manner, that they seem to be a kind of play. And they are very amusing. There is one characteristic of *rakugo* that I like very much. It often has a surprising and funny ending.

Thirdly, in modern variety shows there are often pairs of amusing characters called *manzai*. They come on during the show and keep the audience amused with their funny talk. But their purpose in making people laugh is too obvious.

Personally I much prefer the older sense of humour in *rakugo*, and even in *kyogen*.

Chapter Thirteen
What They Want

"What do the Japanese want?" This is a question that is arising today in all parts of the world. Everywhere people see Japanese cars, Japanese cameras, Japanese TV sets, Japanese washing machines, Japanese everything. "Who are these Japanese?" they ask in surprise. And then, "What on earth do they want?"

The obvious answer is "Money". After all, why does anyone sell anything? Clearly, to make money. There are too many Japanese living together in Japan. Japan is a mountainous country; she has too little space for so many people to live and grow food for themselves. They have to do business abroad, or die. That is the basic fact of life in Japan today.

"But surely Japanese companies do much more business than they really need. Couldn't they be satisfied with a half, or a quarter, and still be well off?''

Well, the making of money isn't their only motive. They are no longer fighting to survive in a hard world. That may have been their motive in the difficult years after the war, about the time I arrived in Japan. But it is their motive no longer. Some other motive has taken its place. What is it?

Now I am speaking no longer of Japanese workers one by one. I am speaking of their companies. The workers are working not so much for themselves and their families, but more for their companies. In working for the group as a whole, they forget themselves. The companies may seem to be modern, in outward appearance. But the spirit behind them is as old as Japan. The warriors of yesterday are the workers of today, and their lord is now the head of the company.

''What then,'' you may ask, ''is the motive of these companies in their search for success? Why are they always making new and better models of all they produce? And why are they always trying to sell them everywhere in the world?''

I can think of three possible motives, and there may well be more. The first is still money. But it is money not for spending but for saving. That may be a strange thing to say. But money is power. If you have a large amount of money in the bank, you can do whatever you like. But if you have nothing, you can't do anything.

The big companies in Japan indeed have a lot

of power. The more money they have in the bank, the more power they have in the world. And so it is business, not politics, that governs the country. And Japanese business is beginning to govern the world as well.

Secondly, businessmen don't act together. Most of the time they act as rivals to each other. It is a kind of race in which they are all running; and each is trying to be first. Sometimes they even push their rivals out of the race.

And thirdly, the Japanese think of themselves not only as members of their company, but also as citizens of their nation. In their minds their company may come first. But in their hearts they desire the honour of their country, too. For honour has always been an important motive of the Japanese.

So the Japanese have steadily aimed at first place in the world, ever since they opened their country to the West in the nineteenth century. When Commodore Perry forced the Japanese to trade with the West, he little realised how much trouble he was making for future ages, both for the West and for Japan. Since then the Japanese have become rivals to all the Western nations. They failed in the war, but today they are close to success, by the more peaceful means of commerce.

These motives aren't present in all Japanese all the time. The Japanese character isn't so simple.

Money, power, competition, honour – these are the motives of Japanese with a strong sense of Duty. Yes, Duty (with a capital D) is a strong force in the minds and hearts of the Japanese, not one by one but as a group. Each one alone would like to go against this sense of Duty. But when they are in a group, they can't oppose it. It is too strong for them. They can only bow down before it.

Still, there are other Japanese with a weaker sense of Duty. They are less connected with any obvious group, such as a business company. They may be writers. They may be teachers. They may be students. Or they may be entertainers. In most cases, they have been under Western influence during their years of training. So they have learned to see things in a different way from most Japanese.

In these Japanese, it is the motive of Pleasure that guides their thoughts and actions. I don't mean that they all look for Pleasure in the same way. But they disagree with those other Japanese who follow their sense of Duty. They say it is this sense of Duty that is destroying their country.

This is what I myself can see, whenever I leave Tokyo and travel through the countryside of Japan. Everywhere the beautiful Japanese countryside of thirty years ago is fast disappearing. Instead, the land is being used for factories, or for houses, or for roads or railways.

Or perhaps the land just isn't needed any more. The Japanese today don't eat so much rice as they used to do. Most of their food comes from abroad. They don't need the rice, and so they don't need the rice fields, either.

"Yes, there is a price to pay for everything. You may follow your sense of Duty; but then you have to give up all idea of Pleasure, and the joy of life."

This is the point of view of those Japanese who prefer to stay at home and follow the ways of Pleasure. What are these ways? On the surface, they may seem to be (once more) the ways of the West. The world of entertainment is very much influenced by the West. Games of baseball and tennis, rock music concerts – they are all Western forms of entertainment. And younger Japanese eagerly follow these ways. For them they are new, modern, exciting. And they give keen pleasure to those who follow them – for a time.

But then, as the Japanese grow older, these ways no longer satisfy them. They come to look back with longing to the ways of the past, the ways of old Japan. They can't help the opening of Japan to the West. It's too late to change that now. But they wish it hadn't happened. For them, everything good has come to them from the old Japan. This old Japan still exists, but it is fast disappearing. So they try to keep as much of it as they can; at least in their memories, in their writings, and in their teaching. I feel sympathy for them.

Now I say: here are two types of Japanese. One is strong; but by his strength he is destroying his country for the sake of money and power. The other is weak; and in his weakness he can't save his country from the destroyer. All he can do is admit defeat. So between them there rises another question. Not "What do the Japanese want?", but "Do they really want anything?"

After all, everything in this world sooner or later passes away. It is what the Japanese themselves deeply realise, and feel even more deeply. They call it the feeling of *mujo*, the sense that nothing remains for long.

Chapter Fourteen
Japan and the World

To me, even after thirty years, Japan still seems a little world of its own. The Japanese themselves are proud of that.

On the other hand, no man can exist for long by himself. And no people can exist for long by themselves, either. When we study the history of

Japan, we find everywhere the influence of China. From early times the writing, the learning, the art, the religion of Japan came from China. It was from China that she learnt the arts of civilisation. When we compare Chinese works of art with those of Japan, it is often difficult to tell the difference. The hand may have been a Japanese hand, but the mind and the heart are so clearly Chinese.

Centuries later the Japanese eagerly followed the example of the West. As before in relation to China, so now in relation to the West, one might say of the Japanese: "Indeed, they are a nation of imitators!"

Even in imitating the West, however, the Japanese kept their sense of national pride. If they imitated the West, it was in order to overtake and defeat the West. As a result of their Westernisation, they went to war with Russia in 1904, and later with England and America in 1941. Now one may say there is a commercial war between Japan and the whole Western world.

But now, I think, the Japanese themselves are beginning to doubt the wisdom of such competition. In going to war with the West, whether with soldiers or traders, they have to follow the ways of the West. So even if they seem to win, they really lose.

So now the Japanese, especially university students, are asking, "How are we to become international?'' Yes, the Japanese today, more than ever before, feel the need of understanding the world, especially the Western world. But they also want the world to understand them. It is a relation that has to work both ways. They realise there is so much for them to understand in the West.

On the other hand, they are afraid that Japan, too, isn't properly understood in Western countries. They want to correct the false picture of Japan they find there. They want to put in its place the true Japan. I admire this way of thinking, and I praise it in my students. To me it offers a bright hope for future relations between Japan and the West. But in it, I still find one weak point: my students are still using the ideas of opposition. On one side is the Japanese nation. On the other side are the Westerners, a mixed group of nations. We may now be friends, instead of enemies, but we remain divided from each other.

For me, the great problem is the group spirit which is so deep in the Japanese character. It was this group spirit which produced the need for international relations between Japan and the West. But it is this same spirit which stands in the way of the only true answer.

In my opinion, the only true answer to this question is to be found neither in Japanese nor in Westerners. I don't say that the Japanese shouldn't know their country better. Rather I want them to do so. Nor do I say that they shouldn't get to know the West a little better. Rather I want them to do so. But I also want them to know and love what is common to the Japanese and all Westerners; and that is our humanity.

This is also what I want Westerners to learn. So it is my hope that the Japanese may come to find their better selves in the West; and that Westerners may come to find their better selves in Japan.

A Word Puzzle

Here are 49 questions for you. The answers are all in this book. Write down the **first letter** of every answer. These letters make a sentence by the English writer John Ruskin.

The Japanese might agree with it. Do you?

1 Funny little drawings in Japan.
2 Hotels with hot springs.
3 Most Japanese have jobs: there is little ______.
4 A Japanese company that makes cars.
5 'The Way of the Eastern Sea'.
6 In Japan, the school year starts in this month.
7 Kyushu is the southern one.
8 Each line of a *haiku* has a fixed ______ of sounds.
9 The oldest religion in Japan.
10 Toshiro Mifune is perhaps the most famous one in Japan.
11 Tatami are ______ -mats.
12 The Japanese navy followed the English ______.
13 Its name means 'the Eastern capital'.

14 An atomic bomb destroyed it.
15 '*Wa*' takes the place of this.
16 The most popular sport in Japan.
17 Japanese study it as a way to get a good job.
18 A shopping street in Tokyo.
19 His family of Tokugawa once ruled Japan.
20 He wrote my first textbook of Japanese.
21 Christianity in Japan spread from its centre here.
22 The Japanese are very ______ in themselves.
23 An old city with brightly painted temples.
24 The world's first great novel was '*The Tale of* ______'.
25 Japanese has no word for 'the' or '______'.
26 There is a huge statue of the Buddha here.
27 If Japanese go on a journey, they like to plan all the ______ first.
28 When Japanese meet, they first bow to ______ other.
29 Japanese businessmen also think of themselves as citizens of their ______.
30 Japanese have a strong sense of ______ to their group.
31 It was once an important commercial centre in the west of Japan.
32 The poisonous blowfish.
33 The month for ghost stories in Japan.
34 When I first arrived in Japan, I studied the Japanese ______ for two years.

35 English writing has ______, but Japanese writing has signs.
36 Japanese television station.
37 The Japanese ______ followed the German example.
38 A way of frying fish and vegetables.
39 The practical Japanese don't have much ______ for English novels and poems.
40 Stories told by a single actor.
41 Mount Fuji is a pile of ______.
42 Shinto is the religion for ______ and marriage.
43 Japanese warriors.
44 Japanese use them to eat food.
45 He used to live in Kyoto.
46 These plays often attract foreign audiences.
47 The Chinese cook for the stomach; the Japanese prepare food for the ______.
48 The Japanese like to eat fish that is still ______.
49 The seaport where we first arrived in Japan.